Cait & Liam

We miss you guys very  hope you will come visit us here in Doha one day.

Tyler can't wait to meet his cousins and would love to show you his big sandpit, the desert :)

Lots of love,

Mari-Bob & Mikke :)

and

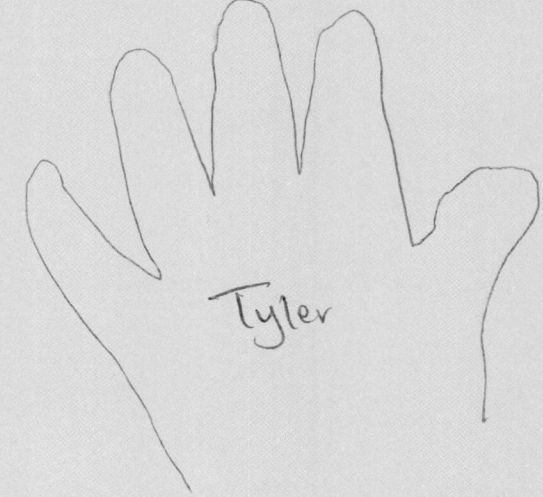

Tyler

Birds of Qatar

First published in 2013 by
Bloomsbury Qatar Foundation Publishing
Qatar Foundation
Villa 3, Education City
PO Box 5825
Doha, Qatar
www.bqfp.com.qa

Text © Frances Gillespie 2013

ISBN 9789992194799

All rights reserved. No part of this publication may be reproduced or transmitted or utilized in any form or by any means, electronic, mechanical, photocopying or otherwise without prior permission of the publisher, nor otherwise be circulated in any form of binding or cover other than in which it is published and without a similar condition being imposed on the subsequent purchaser.

Editor Sindith Kuster
Designer James Watson

Picture credits

Key: t=top, b=bottom, r=right, l=left, c=centre, bg=background
cv=cover, tp=title page

Hanne and Jens Eriksen 8b
Arend Kuester 10/11bg
Dileepkumar Valaparambil Pushpangadhan cv/tr/tl/br/bl, 8/9bg, tp, 10t, 10b, 11t, 11b, 12/13bg, 12b, 13t, 13b,14c, 14b, 15t, 16t, 16b, 17t, 18/19bg, 18c, 19t, 19b, 20/21bg, 20c, 21t, 21b, 22/23bg, 22c, 22b, 23c, 24b, 25b, 26/27bg, 26t, 27t, 30, 32b
Shutterstock 15bg, 24/25bg, 28/29bg

The words in **bold** are explained in the glossary on page 31.

Birds of Qatar

Frances Gillespie

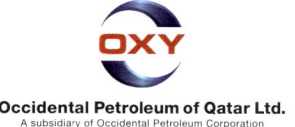

Oxy dedicates the Qatar Nature Explorer books to the children of Qatar.

This series of nature books was developed following our involvement in the Qatar Petroleum Environmental Fair. We were inspired by the tremendous participation of the students of the schools who attend each year and their interest in learning about Qatar's environment.

We hope this set of books will provide value to the Supreme Education Council schools and its students and readers will enjoy learning about the plants, birds, insects and arachnids, mammals, sea and shore life, reptiles and amphibians of Qatar.

Stephen A. Kelly
President & General Manager
Occidental Petroleum of Qatar, Ltd

Contents

Meet the birds	8
Doves and Bulbuls	10
Bee-eaters and Rollers	12
Hoopoes and Parakeets	14
Lagoons, coasts and islands	16
Eagles, Harriers and Ospreys	17
Flamingos, Herons, Egrets and Stilts	18
Gulls, Terns and Cormorants	20
Kingfishers, Moorhens and Ducks	22
Sandy deserts and rocky plains	24
Owls	25
Larks, Wheatears and Shrikes	26
Amazing facts about birds	28
Useful words to know	31
Index	32

Meet the birds

How many birds can you name? There are thousands of birds in the world, with over 500 **species** in the Arabian peninsula. Around 280 species live in Qatar or visit every year. Some are rare, but you can see common birds, like bulbuls and doves, almost every day.

Birds that live in Qatar all year round, such as mynas and parakeets, are called **residents**. Other birds visit Qatar for a few weeks, or even for a few months. They stop over on their long journeys across the world. These journeys are called **migrations**.

MacQueen's Bustard
(*Chlamydotis macqueenii*)

Birds are warm-blooded. Their bones are hollow and light to make it easier to fly. Their legs are covered in scales: hard bits of skin. Birds use their beaks to pick up food. Some, like parrots, can crack nuts in their strong beaks. Birds also use their beaks to tidy their feathers; this is called **preening**. Water birds' beaks have an oil gland to help waterproof their feathers.

Laughing Dove
(Spilopelia senegalensis)

Doves and Bulbuls

The most common doves in Qatar are Laughing Doves and Collared Doves. You will often see them in gardens and parks.

Gardens and farms have plenty of water and this attracts all kinds of birds. These places have seeds and insects for them to eat.

Laughing Doves are small. In the **breeding season** they have pretty pink heads and blue and brown wing feathers. Their name comes from their bubbly cooing, which sounds like laughter.

Red-vented Bulbul
(Pycnonotus cafer)

Collared Doves are slightly bigger. The males and females have a black ring or 'collar' around their neck.

Doves build flimsy nests of twigs in bushes and trees, and even on window-ledges and TV aerials! They lay two white eggs at a time. Unfortunately, the wind sometimes blows the nests down.

White-eared Bulbul
(*Pycnonotus leucotis*)

You can easily recognise White-eared Bulbuls by their black and white heads. They are friendly, noisy garden birds. They call to their reflections in windows and the wing mirrors of cars. Red-vented Bulbuls are shyer and less common. Their black heads have a short crest.

Collared Dove
(*Streptopelia decaocto*)

Bee-eaters and rollers

Bee-eaters and rollers belong to the same group of birds. They have brightly coloured feathers and loud calls.

Bee-eaters eat bees and are not popular with bee-keepers! But they also catch other flying insects such as dragonflies, grasshoppers and butterflies. Before they swallow the bees or wasps they remove the stings by hitting the insects on a hard surface.

European Bee-eater (*Merops apiaster*)

Bee-eaters live in small flocks. They circle high in the sky on their pointed wings, hunting for insects. You usually hear their sweet 'croop croop' calls before you see them. When they perch on a TV aerial, wire or tree branch you can see their wonderful colours.

European Rollers have a blue head, an orange back and bright blue wing feathers. They get their name from the way they sometimes roll over when they fly.

Bee-eaters and rollers eat insects. They hunt in parks, gardens and on farms. You can see them perched on wire fences, waiting to fly up and seize their prey.

Blue-cheeked Bee-eater *(Merops persicus)*

European Roller *(Coracias garrulus)*

Hoopoes and Parakeets

Hoopoes are handsome birds with an orange body and black and white wings. Their name comes from their call, 'hoo-poop-poop'. They have a long crest of feathers, tipped with black. They raise their crests when they land, or when they are excited or alarmed. Hoopoes use their long, sharp bills to dig in the ground for grubs and ants.

Hoopoe
(Upupa epops)

Parakeets are a kind of parrot. They are noisy birds and fly very fast, screaming as they go. They live in small flocks and usually perch near the tops of tall trees.

They love to eat ripe dates, and one of their favourite foods is sunflower seeds.

Rose-ringed Parakeet *(Psittacula krameri)*

Did you know?

In the Holy Qu'ran it says that the Hoopoe carried a message from King Solomon to the land of the Queen of Sheba

Osprey
(Pandion haliaetus)

Lagoons, coasts and islands

Qatar has no natural lakes or rivers. But there are **lagoons** of fresh water and marshy areas, created by people, all over the country. These areas attract thousands of birds. Lagoons have thick beds of reeds where birds like Moorhens and Reed Warblers can hide and build nests.

Qatar is a small **peninsula** but it has a very long coastline. When you go to the beach you will see sea and shore birds wading, flying or diving. There are some small islands, which are flat and sandy, where cormorants and terns nest. In bad weather, their nests can sometimes get flooded by high tides.

Greater Spotted Eagle
(Aquila clanga)

Eagles, Harriers and Ospreys

Lagoons attract wading and swimming birds. They also attract birds of prey. Greater Spotted Eagles circle on their wide wings, watching for the chance to grab a small bird, mammal or even a toad. Eagles will also eat **carrion**: the decaying bodies of dead animals.

Marsh Harriers glide silently just above the reed beds. Sometimes they soar high into the air with their **primary feathers** spread out like fingers.

Ospreys are also **raptors**, like eagles and harriers, but they eat only fish. Their sharp eyes can spot a fish swimming just below the surface of the water. They swoop down and grab the fish in their powerful talons.

Marsh Harrier (*Circus aeruginosus*)

Did you know?

Ospreys build enormous nests of twigs. In some countries they nest at the top of tall trees, but in Qatar they have to nest on the ground

Flamingoes, Herons, Egrets and Stilts

There are forests of mangrove trees around the coast of Qatar. Mangroves grow with their roots in salt water. They provide shelter for the **flocks** of Greater Flamingoes that feed in the shallow water. Flamingoes are wading birds, with long legs and necks. They have pink and white feathers. When a flock is in the air it looks like a long pink ribbon. Flamingoes feed with their heads upside down, and sieve tiny water creatures through their beaks.

Little Egret
(Egretta garzetta)

Grey Heron
(*Ardea cinerea*)

Herons also have long legs. Grey Herons are very common birds. You often see them near the Doha Corniche. They stand very still in the water, and then make a sudden stab at their prey with their long, sharp beaks.

Egrets belong to the same family as herons, and have pure white feathers.

Flocks of Black-winged Stilts live in the lagoons. They are beautiful black and white birds with long, thin, bright pink legs.

Black-winged Stilt
(*Himantopus himantopus*)

Did you know?

Reef Herons sometimes dance about in the water to disturb small fish!

Gulls, Terns and Cormorants

Gulls are mostly white, grey and black, with strong beaks. They have webbed feet to help them to swim. Slender-billed Gulls and Black-headed Gulls are common winter visitors, living in flocks. They are noisy, quarrelsome birds. Gulls catch fish but they are also **scavengers**, fighting for scraps of food that are thrown from boats or washed up on the beach. They can glide for hours on their long, strong wings.

Great Black-headed Gull
(*Larus ichthyaetus*)

Caspian Tern
(*Hydroprogne caspia*)

Terns live in the same **habitat** as gulls. They have pointed wings and forked tails, and their beaks are like daggers. They hover high above the water. Then they suddenly fold their wings and dive into the sea to catch fish.

Terns scream loudly if their nests are in danger. If humans go too near the nests, terns will attack with their sharp beaks. Caspian Terns are the biggest and fiercest of all. Their beaks are bright red.

Sometimes you may see a large flock of black cormorants. They are large, fish-eating birds. Socotra Cormorants dive for fish from a sitting position on the sea. They feed in big groups, and the birds at the back constantly leapfrog over the others in front.

Great Cormorant
(*Phalacrocorax carbo*)

Kingfishers, Moorhens and Ducks

Look for kingfishers where there are mangroves and reed beds. The Common Kingfisher has a brilliant blue head and wings and an orange body. It zips over the water like an electric blue spark. Its large, sharp beak helps it to grab a fish when it dives into the water. Pied Kingfishers sometimes visit lagoons in winter. After catching a fish they can eat it while flying.

Common Kingfisher
(Alcedo atthis)

Pied Kingfisher
(Ceryle rudis)

Moorhens make untidy nests among the reeds. They swim in large flocks and are quarrelsome birds, splashing and chasing each other. The chicks look like balls of black fluff swimming behind their mother.

Male Mallards have a green head and two curly tail-feathers. The females are brown. Female Mallards quack loudly but the males are usually silent. Some kinds of duck search just below the surface for water weeds. Other ducks dive deep to look for weeds, insects and even small fish.

Mallard
(Anas platyryhnchos)

Common Moorhen
(Gallinula chloropus)

Sandy deserts and rocky plains

Not many birds live in the desert. There is no water there and few plants. But some birds actually prefer these wide, empty spaces and the lonely, rocky hills. Insect-eating birds can usually find something to eat. Plenty of flying and crawling insects such as small flies and ants live in the desert.

Eagle Owl (*Bubo ascalaphus*)

Owls

Eagle Owls are among the world's largest owls. They have light brown plumage, ear tufts and large orange eyes that help them see in the dark. They fly silently over the desert at night, hunting for small birds, rodents and insects. A large beetle can be a tasty snack for an owl!

Little Owls start hunting late in the day. They rest during the daytime in dark places like small caves, deserted buildings and even holes in the ground. Little Owls often live and hunt in small family groups. When they are alarmed they hiss and bob their heads up and down.

Owls swallow their prey whole. Later they cough up the bones, feathers, fur and claws as **pellets**. Look for pellets in places where owls have rested during the day. White splashes on rocks or stones are good clues. Wearing gloves, you can gently pull a pellet apart to see what the owl has been eating.

Little Owl
(Athene noctua)

Hoopoe-Lark
(Alaemon alaudipes)

Larks, Wheatears and Shrikes

Hoopoe-Larks and Crested Larks are common insect-eating desert birds. Hoopoe-Larks are slim and a sandy brown. When they fly you can see a black and white band on their wings. These larks seem curious about humans, and often come near people who are walking or picnicking.

Crested Larks are small, with round bellies and a conspicuous spiky crest. They have a sweet, fluting song.

Did you know?

Shrikes are sometimes called 'butcher birds' because they spike surplus food on thorns and twigs as a food store, so that they can come back and eat it later

Wheatears are restless little birds, always on the move. Each species of wheatear has a different black and white tail pattern. Desert Wheatears are handsome birds with a black face mask and a black patch on the wings. They perch on bushes and posts, looking out for insects. Their favourite food is caterpillars.

Crested Lark
(*Galerida cristata*)

Grey Shrikes live on the edge of deserts as well as on farms and in oases. They are aggressive birds, and will hunt insects, small birds, lizards, and even snakes!

Great Grey Shrike
(*Lanius excubitor*)

Amazing facts about birds

Birds are descended from dinosaurs! The earliest birds had teeth and looked like flying lizards

The world's smallest bird is the Bee Hummingbird from Cuba. It weighs only 1.6 grammes

A bird's feathers weigh more than its skeleton

Penguins can dive as deep as 266 metres underwater and stay down for up to 18 minutes

The heaviest flying bird in the world is the Kori Bustard from Africa. Some weigh as much as 19 kilos

Every year, Arctic Terns migrate from the Arctic to the Antarctic and back. This is a journey of around 77,000 kilometres

One of the rarest birds in the world is the Spix's Macaw. It is extinct in the wild, but is being successfully bred in captivity in Qatar

The pink colour of flamingoes comes from the tiny sea creatures they eat

African Ostriches are the world's largest birds. They stand over 2.5 metres tall. A long time ago there were wild ostriches in Qatar

The world's fastest flying bird is the Peregrine Falcon, which can dive on its prey at speeds of up to 350 kilometres per hour

Useful words to know

breeding season the time of year when animals mate and give birth

camouflage the natural colours of an animal that help it to blend into its surroundings

carrion the decaying flesh of a dead animal

flock a group of birds

habitat the natural home of an animal

lagoon a small freshwater lake, or a stretch of sea water that is almost separated from the sea

mammal a warm-blooded animal that has four legs and hair or fur

migration movement from one country or region to another

pellets a small mass of bones, feathers or fur that is coughed up by a bird of prey

peninsula a piece of land that is almost surrounded by water

preen to tidy feathers by using the beak

prey an animal that is hunted or killed for food

primary feathers the strong flight feathers at the end of a bird's wing

raptor bird of prey

resident an animal that lives in the same place all year round

rodent a mammal belonging to a group whose front teeth keep on growing throughout their lives

secondary feathers the feathers along the edge of a bird's wing

species animals that belong to the same group

talons the sharp claws of a bird of prey

Index

bee-eater 12-13
bulbul 8, 10-11
cormorant 16, 20-21
dove 8, 10-11
duck 22-23
eagle 16-17
egret 18-19
flamingo 18, 29
gull 20-21
harrier 17
heron 18-19
hoopoe 14-15
hoopoe-lark 26
insect 10, 12-13, 23-27

kingfisher 22
lark 26-27
moorhen 16, 22-23
myna 8
osprey 16-17
owl 24-25
parakeet 8, 14-15
reed warbler 16
roller 12-13
shrike 26-27
stilt 18-19
tern 16, 20-21, 29
wheatear 26-27